Cromosys Publication

ENGLISH DICTIONARY of MODERN SLANG

NIRANJAN JHA SHOWMAN

Founder - Niranjan Jha Showman

Education and Technology Research Center

Patankar Park, Nallasopara (W), Mumbai. +91-9561450045

Education, Technology, Publication, Healthcare, Newsmedia, Realtor, Filmmaking

www.facebook.com/cromosys

+91-9561450045
Learn Advanced Skills
And Get Job Instantly
GERMAN
Python
FRENCH
C++
SPANISH
Java
ENGLISH
HTML5
RUSSIAN
CSS
JavaScript
Cromosys
Education and Technology Research Center
Nallasopara (W), Mumbai

Learn Web Programming
Demo-Class Free
HTML
CSS
React
JavaScript
Typescript
Bootstrap
Cromosys
20 Years of Experience
Nallasopara (W), Mumbai
+91-9561450045

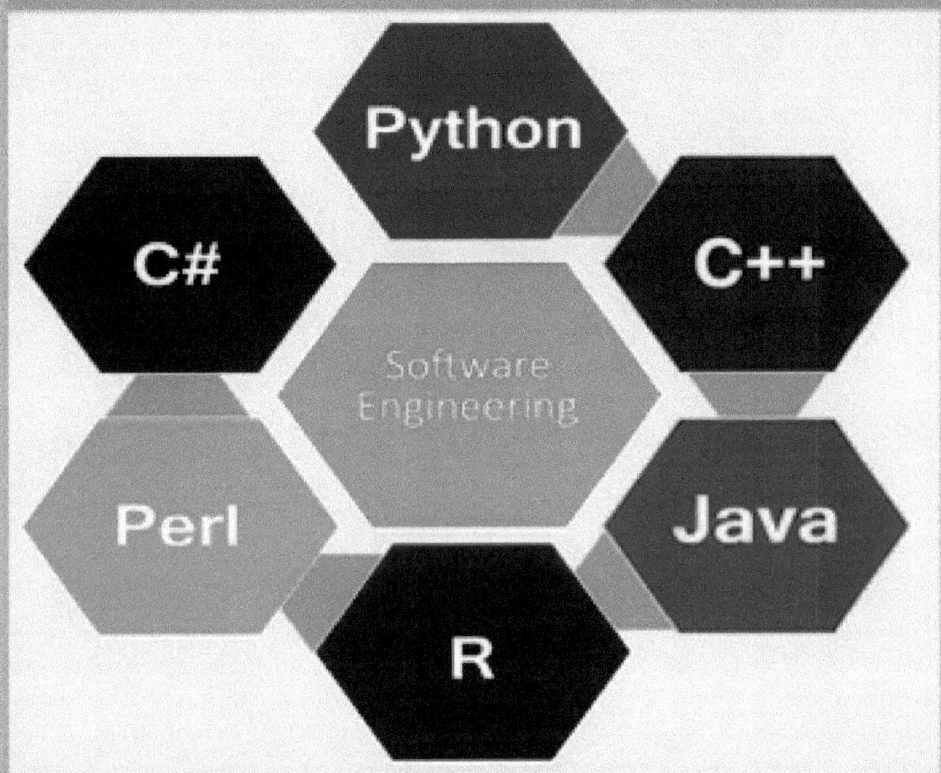
+91-9561450045
Learn Software Engineering
Demo-Class Free
Python
C#
C++
Software
Engineering
Perl
Java
R
Cromosys
20 Years of Experience
Nallasopara (W), Mumbai
+91-9561450045

25 Years of Experience
Learn Visual Multimedia
Animation VFX
Movie Editing
Game Development
Cromosys
+91-9561450045
Education and Technology Research Center
Nallasopara (W), Mumbai
www.facebook.com/cromosys

Jobs Available
For Candidates Who Know

German

French

Spanish

Vacancy in Germany, France, Spain
For Hospitality, Engineering, IT Sector
With Free Visa, Airfare and Accommodation

Cromosys
Education and Technology Research Centre
Nallasopara (W), Mumbai
+91-9561450045
20 Years of Experience

+91-9561450045
Foreign Languages Institute
German, French, Spanish
Basic and Advanced - All Levels
3 x 6 = 18 Courses
FRANCHISE
Business Offer
Teaching Materials Provided
We have 1 Million Students Globally
Great Income Assured
Global Exposure
Cromosys
20 Years of Experience
Nallasopara (W), Mumbai
+91-9561450045

Cromosys Publication

English Dictionary of Modern Slang

Niranjan Jha Showman

Preface

Cromosys Publication's **English Dictionary of Modern Slang** book is an optimal quality guide to the beginners as well as advanced learners of English slang. This is an unmatchable and unique book of its kind that guarantees your success in terms of getting acquainted to the modern usage of slang words in current era. You may have seen many other books on slang but most of them are outdated and of no use because their junk of unacceptable, profane, and bad words creates a nuisance in English. Some lexicographers don't know that there is a difference between slang and nonsense, and everything what is nonsense can not be brought into the social circumference of a language. Considering that point, giving best effort to this venture, this book is created as a profound compilation of new, accepted and nearly acceptable words with their unique established meaning for today's world. Giving utmost attention and care, spending fifteen years in research, we have harbored those words which are meaningful and having a base in the slang world. Being the best reference for the entire globe, this book holds its significance of being dynamic, systemic, lucid and blissful with pure and perfect arrangement of words with their meaning written in the easiest way. This book is highly useful for the people working in communication based industry, media houses, entertainment world, and for those who are teachers, writers, researchers and students. And definitely for those who love languages – especially English!

First of all, I have to make it clear what is slang. Slang is a colorful and alternative vocabulary that bristles with humor, vituperation, prejudice, and informality. The slang of English is English with its sleeves rolled up, its shirts-tails dangling, and its shoes covered in mud. This dictionary presents a panoramic view of twentieth-century English slang – from Britain, America, Australia, and elsewhere in English-speaking world from 1950 until 2013. After spending more than a decade in research, I am convinced to say that in today's world the people should have the knowledge of English slang also. One alone, being immaturely suggested, spend ages in watching movies and listening to the audio which helps them to imitate a little but not learn what in actual sense it is, and their never-ending process of Picasso Adventure collects some scattered information which is unworthy linguistic approach. And the aspirants get lost in wilderness. The world's attitudes to the use of language have changed greatly over the last three decades, and the perceived boundaries between standard and unorthodox are becoming increasingly fuzzy, and so, slang is accepted and even in some cases embraced and promoted by mainstream society. Today, tabloid newspapers in the UK such as the Sun, the Star and the Sport regularly use slang in headlines and articles, while the quality press use slang sparingly – usually for special effect – but the assumption remains that readers have a working knowledge of common slang terms. A vast majority of people have come to see slang as their own common language, in which they are fluent, and which may therefore take precedence over the other varieties in their repertoires. The use of slang forms part of what linguists call code-switching or style-shifting or the mixing of and moving between different languages, dialects or codes.

Cromosys Publication's *English Dictionary of Modern Slang* is to bring you into the light of the thorough usage of English Slang incorporated through the American, British and Australian vocabulary. The terms are dealt with a lucid manner with reference to the perfect understanding for all levels. It contains the words of twentieth century which are clear and have obtained a substantial foothold in the language. One thing is necessary to say that the vocabulary of slang changes rapidly: what is new and existing for one generation is old-fashioned for the next. Old slang often either drifts into obsolescence or become accepted into the standard language, losing its eccentric color. Flapper, for instance, started life in the late nineteenth century as a slang term for a young unconventional or lively woman, but subsequently moved into the general language as a specific term for such a young woman of the 1920s. The pace of change in the usage of slang is curious in its own right, and is an aspect which I want to highlight in this dictionary. On occasions, slang can be offensive, because it singles out the particular group of people in an insulting or condescending way. The English language is not always politically correct, and so, my view to this is that however regrettable this aspect of English may be, its inclusion in a dictionary of slang doesn't sanction its must-use, but simply records the facts as far as they are available.

Cromosys, our education and technology research center, saving human efforts from being wasted, is to educe human civilization to educational luminosity. The world growing with density has brought enormous opportunity to the people who have a good knowledge of English irrespective of their geographical boundaries. Having been teaching this language for last several years, I have come across the numerous words which I have listed in this book. Our path-breaking pioneer training institute for English Speaking, Mass Communication, Foreign Languages, Computer Training, and Competition Coaching, is committed to enlightening human mind with educational endeavors, and we are doing the same for last successful fifteen years. I believe I have done all I could to make this book useful to you, and not only hopeful but I am sure that your success is in your hand now because this book will take you miles ahead in your expectation. We always respect the views and comments of readers, so for any communication with regards to assistance, enquiry or collaboration, we are always there at your reach as it helps us improve our ability.

Niranjan Jha Showman
Trainer, Author Physician, Entrepreneur, Filmmaker, Activist
Founder of Cromosys Corporation
facebook.com/cromosys
+91-9561450045
cromosys@yahoo.com
Nallasopara (W), Mumbai, India

My other books: -
English Voice Accent and Pronunciation
Teach Yourself German
Teach Yourself French
Teach Yourself Spanish
Be millionaire like me
Dynamic Grammar of English
Teach Yourself HTML5
Teach Yourself 3ds Max
Teach Yourself Autodesk Maya

Cromosys Corporation
Education and Technology Research Center
Education, Technology, Publication, Healthcare, Realtor, Filmmaking
facebook.com/cromosys
+91-9561450045
cromosys@yahoo.com
Nallasopara (W), Mumbai, India

About the Author

Niranjan Jha Showman
Trainer, Author, Physician, Entrepreneur, Filmmaker, Activist

Niranjan Jha Showman is a Language Scientist and Technical Researcher. He is the Award Winning author of more than fifty educational and fictional books at Amazon. He is one of the great-grandsons of the first President of India Dr. Rajendra Prasad. He is a Public Figure, and the globally - renowned Languages Trainer of French, Spanish, and German from past twenty years. Niranjan Jha Showman is an Entrepreneur and also works as a Filmmaker in India. Being the founder and owner of Cromosys Corporation - a company located in Mumbai, India, his company is excelling in the fields of Education, Technology, Publication, Newsmedia, Realtors, Banking, and Cinemascope from past fifteen years.

Niranjan Jha Showman's good-seller educational books and novels are appreciated worldwide. He has more than one million eBook buyers online, and more than one million learners are connected to him globally. One of his novels is critically acclaimed. He is the trainer of French, Spanish, German, English Voice and Accent, and Advanced Computer Education. He is also a political activist in India.

Niranjan Jha Showman is the man who came from rags to riches, he who knows how to turn the table, and he, whom you call the man of Midas-touch. He has observed lives from the Pandora of monkeys to the sanctuary of monks, not only down-to-earth but down-to-grave. He is a B. Com. graduate, and B. Ed. from Delhi University, and diploma holder in French, Spanish and German from America. You can watch his songs, movies, educational videos and many more things by typing "Niranjan Jha Showman" in Google.

Niranjan Jha Showman
+91-9561450045
cromosys@yahoo.com
Mumbai, India
facebook.com/cromosys

Statutory

This book with its content is the registered property of the author Niranjan Jha Showman.
The author and his Cromosys Publication holds all necessary rights of this book.
The copyright certificate of this book is attached at the end of this book.

A

Absoblutely: Absolutely (In emphatic sense)

Accident: A child whose conception was not planned by their parents

Ace boon: A best friend of yours

Acid house: A place where people take drugs

AC-DC: A man who is sexually attracted by the persons of either sex, also called 'ambisextrous'

Acid test: A severe test that you apply to examine or find out the truth of something

Action gagnée: A successful and joyful sexual intercourse (Pronounced – action gagnee)

Action duplex: A sexual act involving both vaginal and anal sex

ABC sex: Sex only on anniversaries, birthdays and Christmas

Afroginist: The black people from African origin who support back-racism and contradict Zionist attitude in America [Blend of Afro and originist]

Afterthought: The younger child in a family who is born considerably later than the other children

Aggro: An aggressive person

Air jerk: Making a motion with hands to express disgust, disinterest or disbelief while rolling eyes

Airlocked: Drunk, intoxicated

Airy-fairy: A person who is lacking in strength of character

Alan Whickers: Knickers, underwear

Alaskan Firedragon: A sexual activity in which a man ejaculates on the face of his partner

Alf: A derogatory term for the uneducated and unthinkingly conservative Australian

Alislut: A woman who has the intention of getting married to a rich man and then seeking divorce to accumulate money [Contraction of alimony and slut]

Alley cat: A prostitute who keeps roaming around the streets frequently

Alltheist: A person with such a broad spiritual views that he respects all the religions

Alkie: An alcoholic, especially one who lives rough or frequents the streets

Alligator: A fan of jazz or swing music

All there: A mentally-alert person (adjective)

Alpha dog: A head of the family who dominates his family members

Alpha geek: The most technically proficient and knowledgeable member of a group

Altar tapism: 1.The selfish motive of some religious people to occupy the entire world. 2. The tendency of some religious people to use their shrine for their own gratification

Ambisextrous: A man who is sexually attracted by the persons of either sex

Ambulance chaser: The one who takes benefits from others' misfortune

Anilingus: The sexual act of licking or kissing the anus in lovemaking [Blend of anal and cunnilingus]

Ankle biter: A young child who disturbs their parent for small things

Anork: The one who is absurd and unfashionable by his nature

Antwacky: Old fashioned (Pronounced – aantwaki)

A-OK: In a perfect order or condition (adverb)

Ape: A sexually aggressive man

Apple polisher: A person who treats others with special kindness so that he can get help

Arbiter: A person appointed to work as a mediator to settle a dispute

Arch-slave: The woman in religious service who is being sexually exploited by their male leaders

Aristocratism: The doctrine in India to defeat communism and its radical naxal activities

Arm candy: A physically attractive companion who is working as a bodyguard or escort to a celebrity or influential person

Arse-licker: A sycophant who treats others with special kindness so that he can get help

Arse-man: A man whose favorite part of a woman's anatomy is the buttocks

Arty-farty: A person who pretends to be an artist

Arvo: afternoon

Aastala vista: See you again, good bye (Spanish word)

Askhole: Someone who asks many stupid, pointless, and obnoxious questions

Ass bandit: A man more inclined to have anal sex than vaginal, also called 'sodomite'

Ass chaser: A man looking for news girls to go bed with

Asset beauty: A beautiful woman with good-shaped buttocks

Aunt flow: Menstruation

Aussie kiss: An activity of kissing or licking sexual organs. Also called 'blow job, cunnilingus, fellatio, carpet munching'

Awright: An alternative spelling and pronunciation of alright

B

Babbler: Someone who talks too much and opens some secrets which he should not do

Babelicious: Very sexually attractive

Babe magnet: A male person who is very smart in attracting girls

Babia-majora: An extremely attractive woman

Bach: A man who is willing to live as a bachelor

Bachelorette: A single British woman

Backdoor: To commit adultery with (verb)

Backhander: A bribe or secret payment made to gain some benefits

Backroom boys: The people who do important work for a person or an organization but the public do not know about them

Back passage: Anus

Back slang: The language spoken using the words or letters backwards, like – instead of *'boy'* you speak *'yob'*

Backsnurging: The act of sexual pleasure when a man sniffs or smells female underwear

Backseat driver: The one who criticizes others without responsibility

Backy Fiona: A girl who has well-grown and round buttock which makes her look beautiful and attractive

Bad hair day: A day when you feel that everything is going wrong with you and that is making you upset and annoyed

Baloney: Nonsense

Barebacking: Anal sex without condom

Bad-mouth: to criticize (verb)

Bail bandit: Someone who commits a crime while on bait awaiting a trial

Balderdash: Nonsense

Ball and chain: A man's wife

Bald-headed hermit: The penis

Ballsy: The one who is courageous and powerful

Banker's ramp: A conspiracy by bankers to engineer a financial crisis in order to damage the standing of a government to which they are inimical

Basket: A child who is born to unmarried parents

Basket case: A country which is in bad economical condition with no possibility to come up

Bazookas: The large breasts of a woman

Battleaxe: A domineering woman

B-boy: A participant in hip hop street culture

Beach-bum: A person devoted to spending as much time as available on the beach

Beaver: The female sexual organ and surrounding area

Bedroom eyes: The way of looking at someone with the intention of having physical relation (Noun)

Beer belly: A punch developed by drinking large quantities of beer

Beer goggles: The effect of alcohol when one finds others more sexually attractive (Noun)

Bejesus: Expressing surprise or annoyance

Belly button: The navel

Belly-laugh: A deep uncontrollable laugh

Beltway bandit: A private company that hires a person who was previously employed in government agencies, so that the company can get some government contacts

Bevvy: A general term for an alcoholic drink

B girl: A woman employed at shop to encourage customers to buy more

Bi: Bisexual

Bible basher: The one who speaks a lot about the Bible or Christianity

Bible pounder: A person who follows the instructions of the Bible in a vigorous and aggressive manner

Big bucket: A woman who looks ugly because of her exceptionally big buttock

Big-mouth sister: If a man calls a woman his sister just to show to the people but goes in physical relation with her, so that woman is his 'big-mouth sister'

Big Apple: New York city

Big girl's blouse: A man with no physical strength

Billy no-mates: A person who has no friends

Bimbo: A woman who is young and beautiful but behaves like a child

Biscuit shooter: A waitress

Bitch slap: A stinging slap or blow to humiliate someone

Blabbermouth: A speaker who reveals too much

Black bomber: The drug to stimulate for sex

Black velvet: An attractive woman of black color

Bleaker: The parents, especially a father who persuades his daughters to become a call-girl

Blockfig: Your girlfriend's lover [Contraction of blocking figure]

Blooming lunatic: A highly educated but stupid person

Blop strop: The tension of a woman related to her menstruation problem

Blow job: Fellatio or cunnilingus that involves kissing and licking of sexual organs

Blue waffles: A severe infection on the vagina with too much of burning because of excessive intercourse

Blue ball: The extreme sexual frustration of a man (Noun)

Blue blank: The depression causing madness

Blue-carpet boss: A boss who persuades his female employees for lovemaking

Blue-chip investment: The investment that you think is safe and will make a profit

Blue-eyed boy: Your favorite person whom you treat with special favor

Blue-line bonker: A man inclined to make love to very young girls of his age

Bludger: A pimp

Blue funk: A state of extreme fear or terror

Blue-grapes: The physical relation between a husband and wife occurring very rarely because of lack of interest. In sentence: *He is giving me some blue-grapes, nothing else.*

Blue slave: A woman who works in a hotel as a waitress cum prostitute

Bluestocking: A well-educated woman, who is more interested in ideas and studying than in traditional old fashioned things related to woman only

Bobfoc: A female with attractive body but ugly face (Pronounced – bobfok)

Bolbachan: A boastful statement

Bolshy: An uncooperative person

Bomb shell: A very attractive and sexy woman

Boffstation: A prostitute house, a brothel

Bone-belt: A black magician seeking sexual favor from his female followers

Bonkbuster: A book or film characterized by frequent sexual encounters between the characters

Booby rampage: The sexual activity of a woman rubbing her breasts with male genital, also called 'Dutch sex'

Booty bandit: A man who commits male rape

Boozehound: Drunkard

Botch job: A makeshift construction or repair of something that is going to fail in a long run

Bottler: The one who easily gives up or loses his courage to complete a task

Boyfriend drop: When you propose a girl but she refuses telling a lie to you that she already has a boyfriend, so this activity of her is called 'boyfriend drop'

Brainiac: Very intelligent person

Bracket busy: A mentally upset or frustrated person who pretends to be busy but the fact is that he has lost his interest to do any work

Brass monkey weather: Extremely cold weather

Brat pack: A group of film stars enjoying a rowdy or fun-loving lifestyle

Brazilian cold: A mental disorder in which you feel very annoyed when somebody reminds you something unpleasant

Bread basket: Stomach

Breadhead: A person who is obsessed with making money

Brewer's droop: A temporary impotence as a result of drinking excessive amount of alcohol

Broad: A prostitute

Broken mirror: (1) A superstition or blind belief which is still being followed by the people. (2) Poverty

Broken-mirror stress: The heavy stress of extreme poverty (Noun)

Brolly: An umbrella

Brother of broadway: A man who behaves decently showing brotherly affection to a woman but his true intention is to develop romantic relationship

Brouhaha: A useless commotion

Brown-collar job: The job of a soldier

Brown envelop: The thing that is full of confusion

Brown-nose: The one who praise other or behave sycophantically

Brunch: The food that you eat in the late morning as a combination of breakfast and lunch

Bubblehead: An empty headed and stupid person

Buffer guest: A friend of yours who you call in a party just to show to the other guests that the party is already started when they come

Bugger: An anal sex lover

Bull-dyke: A lesbian with masculine tendencies

Bum-bag: A small pouch worn around the waist or hips, held in place by a strap or belt, and used to hold valuables and money

Bum-boy: A male prostitute

Bum-chum: A person with an apparently overly close friendship

Bumshot: Anal sex

Bunker sheltering: The activity of press media when they take bribes from a criminal and protect him by publicizing him innocent

Bunny-boiler: A jealous or obsessive woman whose behavior with her former or intended partner is desperate or dangerous

Bupkis: Nothing at all

Busman's holiday: The holiday that you spent doing the same thing that you do at your work place

Butt crack: The upper part of a woman's buttock that is visible when she bends down because she has worn low-waist and skin-tight clothes

Butter-and-egg man: A wealthy unsophisticated man who spends money freely

Butt pirate: A male homosexual who enjoys sodomy

Button man: Someone who is working for a big criminal or underworld man at a low level

Buy-curious: The one who just looks at a shop but doesn't buy anything

By blow: The child who is born to unmarried parents

C

Cabbaged: A person who is extremely drunk or high on drugs

Calf love: The love of adolescence age

California roll: When you fail to make a complete stop at a red light or stop sign especially at a turn, that is 'California roll'

Camcouple: A married couple who captures the video of their own sexual act to sell online [Contraction of camera-couple]

Camel toe: When a woman is wearing a tight clothe and the front part of thighs and vaginal area appears to be mounding even if they are covered, that is called a 'camel toe'

Caps lock voice: When a normally calm person raises his voice and uses an authoritative tone – that is called caps lock voice

Carpet muncher: A lesbian

Casting couch: A man working for a movie seeking sexual favor from his female associates

Catamite: A passive male homosexual partner

Catbird seat: A superior or advantageous position

Catch-22: A difficult situation when you are not able to escape because you have got two works to do and neither you can do both of the works at once, nor first work before doing second, nor second work before doing first

Cesspool: A place where dishonest and immoral people gather

Chancer: The one who takes chances or does risky things

Chequebook journalism: The activity of press and media house when they desperately look for hot news and they buy it by paying money

Chaser: An amorous pursuer of women

Chasy belt: A woman who has a very strong ill-feeling for sex, and so, she cannot allow a man to go physical with her [Colloquial of chastity belt]

Cheap Charlie: A mean person

Chick magnet: A male person very smart in attracting girls

Chick: A young woman, also called a Chicklet

Chick flick: A film full of girls' poses

Chinaman's chance: A negligible prospect

Chinese whisper: The situation when the information is passed from one person to another but it gets slightly changed each time

Chinese angle: A strange or unusual twist or aspect to something

Chink: A Chinese person

Chinless wonder: A rich person who lacks depth of character and intelligence

Christer: An over-religious person

Chopsocky: A kind of film featuring violent actions involving martial art

Chubby-chaser: A person who finds fat people attractive

Church mouse: A very poor person who begs for living

Ciao: An Italian word used as a greeting at the time of meeting or departing (Pronunciation – chaao)

City slicker: Someone who behaves in a way which is typically city-lifestyle

Cleanskin: Someone with a clean police record

Clean sneak: An escape with no clues left behind

Clever-clogs: An idiot who claims to be clever or have great knowledge, also called 'clever Dick'

Clip-joint: A place of deception

Clippie: A female bus conductor

Cloth-ears: The one who has a poor sense of hearing

Clusterfuck: When a lot of things are going extremely wrong in a short period of time

Clustering: A sexual activity involving three persons, also called sandwich sex

Cock: The penis

Cockpit crunch: A sexual act when there is no appropriate time or place and that makes the situation a little fearful

Cocksman: A man who is considered to be exceptionally skilled in lovemaking

Cock-teaser: A sexually provocative woman, who attracts a man but refuses intercourse at the end, also called 'vagina drop'

Code brown: The condition when your stomach is upset and you are going to toilet again and again, also termed 'Delhi belly'

Cold courage: An advice that is not true but you are giving to someone to console him so that he can come out of the grief

Coldfish: An unemotional or insensitive person

Cold reception: When somebody welcomes you showing happiness but in fact he is not happy and wants you to go as soon as possible, that is – cold reception

Cold turkey: A bad condition of mind when someone feels that his body is shivering and mind is not stable at the time when he has suddenly stopped taking drugs

Columbia shock: A very disturbing feeling perceived by a young man who visits a brothel for the first time and that results no erection on him

Come: The ejaculated semen

Come-on: The signal that a girl can give to encourage someone for lovemaking

Comedy of manners: The behavior of some people when they intend to show that they are happy and they try to make other also happy

Comfort station: The Toilet

Con artist: A cheater

Concrete jungle: A city which has many large modern buildings and no trees or parks

Confidence trick: An act of cheating someone keeping him under confidence

Confrickster: A confidence trickster

Conspicuous consumption: The way of showing richness when one buys expensive things and shows them to the people

Costa del Crime: A place where many fugitive criminals live

Co-respondent: A person who is having sexual relation with the wife or husband of somebody who is trying to get divorce

Couch potato: A person who likes wasting time by sitting at home and watching television

Cowboy: Someone who is careless and dishonest in his work

Cowboy job: The activity of secretly getting important political or military information about another country or finding out another company's secrets by using spies

Crabby: A moody and short tempered person

Crackpot: An impractical person in his behavior because he has some strange and crazy ideas

Cracksman: A thief

Cradle-snatcher: A man who likes to have sex with those who are quite younger than his age

Crash pad: A place for the poor people to sleep

Crawler: A man who tries to get somebody's favor by praising him or doing all that will make him happy

Credibility gap: When you do not do what other people were expecting or you do exactly opposite to what you had said or promised before – is called credibility gap

Creep-house: A brothel or other place where prostitutes rob their clients

Creeping Jesus: A person who shows to others that he is very religious but in fact he is not

Crook: Dishonest or criminal minded

Crown jewels: The male genital organ

Crumb: A person who does not agree with others' opinion that is why he objects all the time

Cubicle coma: When you wake up you feel energized, but when you go to office, a wave of tiredness runs over you, and once you leave your office, you suddenly feel energized and everything seems to be ok – that is called cubicle coma

Cubicle monkey: A desk-bound officer who works too much in his office

Cugar: An old woman looking for a younger boyfriend

Cugine: A young man taking initial steps to get into underworld (Pronounced kyugeen)

Culchie: A rural dweller

Cum droplet: The semen that a male partner ejaculates on the face of his partner

Cunnilingus: The sexual activity when a man kisses or licks the vagina of his female partner

Cunt: Female sexual organ

Cunt-struck: A man who is extremely infatuated with a woman

Cupboard love: The love between two people when they want to gain something because of selfish motives

Curate's egg: A thing that is partly good and partly bad

Curtain lecture: The shouting of a wife to her husband making sure others should not listen to it

Cuckold: 1 A man who likes to see his wife having sex with another man. 2 A man who is the husband of a prostitute

Cut-out: A person who is acting as a mediator in the activity of secretly getting important political or military information about another country or finding out another company's secrets by using spies

Cyberpunk: A young person who is very fond of using internet, computing and information technology

D

Dab hand: A man very good at doing something because he is efficient and well-trained on that

Daisy chain: A sexual activity involving three people, also termed 'threesome'

Dalliance: A relationship between two persons that is not serious and that results a casual love affair

Damp: A man who easily ejaculates seeing beautiful woman because of his weak sexual power

Damp squib: An unsuccessful attempt of yours when you try to impress someone

Dandy: A man who is unnecessarily devoted to style, smartness and fashion

Darby and Joan: A married couple who is old but still loves each

Dark horse: An unpopular person who suddenly becomes famous because of getting success from an unexpected work done by him

Darl: Darling

Daredevil: Someone who enjoys doing dangerous thing in a way that other people may think is stupid

Dark lore: The knowledge or learning related to black magic

Date rape: The crime of raping a girl when the lover calls her on a date

Dating agency: A business center or an organization that arranges meeting between a man and a woman who want to begin a romantic relationship

Dazzle: To impress a person with knowledge or ability or any brilliant display or prospect

Dear John letter: The letter that a woman gives to a man terminating relationship (Noun – *Is she going to give you a Dear John letter?*)

Debonair: A fashionable and confident man

Deb's delight: An attractive young man in high society

Decadent: The person who shows low moral standard and has interest only in pleasure and enjoyment rather than serious things

Decollete: The top edge of a woman's dress that is designed to be very low in order to show her shoulders

Déjà vu: When you feel that you have previously experienced something which is happening to you now – that is déjà vu (Noun)

Delhi belly: An upset stomach compelling you to go to toilet again and again

DT: A physical condition in which people who drink too much alcohol feel their body shaking and imagine they are seeing things which are really not there. (Abbreviation of delirium tremens)

Delusion of grandeur: A belief that you are more important than you actually think about yourself

Demagogue: A political leader who tries to win support by using arguments or rising issues which are very sensitive to religious or emotional view points

Deadpan: A person with no expression or emotion on his face

Death rattle: A gurgling sound that comes out of the throat of a dying person

Debt bored: Someone who is so bored with life that he just spends money to make it more exciting

Decree absolute: The final order for divorce

Demonomania: An abnormal mental state in which a person thinks or behaves like he has got an evil spirit on him

Derelict: Someone who does not have his home or job or even property

Desk rage: The peak of office employees' stress level

Desperado: A person who does dangerous and criminal things without caring for himself or other

Desperate soul: A person who is restless and tensed because he is in the need of something and for that he is bothering others

Deviant: A man with sexually abnormal behavior

Dewy-eyed: A very sentimental person who cries quite often

Diehard: A very persistent and stubborn person

Dicey: A work that is full of risks

Dick: The penis

Dildo: An object shaped like a penis used for sexual pleasure

Dilemma: A situation in which you are confused because you are not able to decide which of two works you should do first

Dinky: A professional working couple who have no children

Dipso: A person with an abnormal desire of drinking a lot of alcohol

Dirty weekend: A weekend that you spend secretly with your lover

Discussion Uganda: A discusses or talks about sex. In sentence – *What the discussion Uganda is going on there?*

Disgawsome: Something which is disgustingly awesome [Contraction of disgustingly awesome]

Disorderly house: A brothel

Displaced anger: When you are angry for some other reason but showing anger on someone or something else

D-notice: A government notice to news editors not to publish items on specified subjects for security reasons. (Abbreviation of defense notice)

Doggy bag: A bag given to a customer in a restaurant to put the leftovers food in it for home

Do-gooder: A well-meaning but unrealistic reformer

Dog's age: A long time. In sentence – *A dog's age has passed since I have seen you.*

Dogwatch: A night shift job especially in a newspaper office

Dolce vita: A life of pleasure and luxury

Doldrums: A period of inactivity or feeling of boredom and depression

Domino effect: The effect when one event causes a sequence of similar events

Dona: A man's sweetheart

Dooms day: The last day of the world when all will die

Dopester: The one who collects information and forecasts the result of a sport, election, etc.

Dot-com dick: Someone who keeps on browsing lot of websites on internet

Double O: An intense look

Double bluff: The truth that somebody spoke to you in such a cunning and persuasive way that you took as a lie but in fact that is truth

Double-cross: An act of deceiving somebody showing that you are helping him

Double Dutch: The language that you can not understand at all

Double faced: Someone who admires you in your presence and bad-mouth when you are absent

Doublethink: The capacity to accept contrary opinions at the same time

Doubling: An insertion with something that results both the vagina and anus being penetrated at a time (Noun)

Doubting Thomas: A person who always doubts

Dough: Money

Dropper: The one who passes counterfeit money

Dry humping: The activity when the two people fully clothed repeatedly keep on rubbing the body on each other especially the genital areas to gain sexual pleasure

DSL: A woman expert in giving blow job to her male partner [Dick sucking lips]

Duff sticking: The activity of a male person when he tries to rub or stick his sexual organ with a standing male or female person in a crowded place

Dullsville: An imaginary place that is extremely dull and boring

Dumbo: Stupid, slow-witted

Dunce: Someone who is very slow at learning

Dutch sex: The sexual activity of a woman rubbing her breasts with her male partner's genital

Dutch act: Suicide

Dutch auction: A sale of goods in which the price is reduced by the auctioneer until a buyer is found

Dutch cap: A contraceptive cap to prevent pregnancy

Dutch courage: The intoxicating effect of alcohol when a person feels elated and speaks too much

Dutch party: A party in which each person makes a contribution to pay the bill

Dutch uncle: A good advisor of yours who advises you at a needful time

Dystopia: A place of your imagination in which you think everything is bad

E

Ear-biter: Someone who always tries to borrow money from you

Early bird: A person who gets up early in the morning

Easy cry: Someone who is so emotional that he cries easily

Easy lady: A call-girl or prostitute

Easy money: The money that you earn easily without putting more efforts

Easy-peasy: Very easy

Easyrich: A person who has become easily rich

Easer-ride: A sexually satisfying lover

Easy touch: A person who can be easily exploited financially

Eaves dropper: Someone who listens to others' private talk secretly (Pronounced – eevz dropr)

Echo chamber: A person who totally agrees with everything another person says

Ecodrums: The financial crisis of a country or the world caused by recession and other problems [Contraction of economical doldrums]

Economic vegetarian: A person who is vegetarian because he can't afford to buy non-vegetarian food

Eden Garden: A place where you can get every thing and enjoy every moment with great happiness

Edutainment: A subject matter of education combined with entertainment

Eff: Fuck

Elbow tag: Your activity when you are sitting in a theater and adjust your posture in such a way that your arm or elbow touches the girl sitting next to you

Electra complex: A mental disorder when a father feels a carnal desire for his own daughter or vice versa

Elopement: The activity of a girl running away with her lover to marry secretly

Emotional dump: The act of throwing emotional crap onto one or more of your friends

Endsville: A place or a situation from where you do not have any further hope

Enforcer: A strong-arm man in an underworld gang

Enigma: The thing that is puzzling you

Epicenter: The central point of something which is creating difficulty

Epicure: A man with refined taste in food and drink

Erotomania: Excessive sexual desire in a man or woman

Erring sister: A prostitute

Escapist: The man who runs away from truth

Espionage: The activity of secretly getting important political or military information about another country or finding out another company's secrets by using spies

E-thug: An internet thug who takes others' money illegally

Eunophilia: The practice of having sex with a eunuch [Contraction of eunuch and philia]

Euphoria: An extremely strong feeling of happiness and excitement of false belief

Ex: A former husband, wife, or lover

Ex benefits: When a man and woman continue their physical relation even after break up or divorce – that is ex benefits

Ex-con: Ex convict – Someone who has been convicted before

Expiration dating: A date and meeting of the lovers who are soon to get separated

Eye shagging: An act of a man to stare at a woman with the imagination of having sexual gratification

Extheist: Someone who believed in God before but now he does not believe

Eye tonic: A girl who you often look at while working in an office for some excitement

Eye-candy: Something visually arresting but intellectually undemanding

F

F-word: An abusive or bad word starting with the letter 'f'

Face-ache: Someone who looks very sad from his face

Face lift: A medical operation in which the skin of a person's face is tightened

Factotum: An employee who does a wide variety of jobs. Someone who performs troublesome duties for another

Fag: A homosexual male person

Fair-weather friend: The one who stops being your friend when you are in trouble

Fait accompli: Something that has already happened and you can not change

Faith healing: A method of treating a sick person through the power of belief and prayer

Fall back: A plan or course of action that is ready to be used in an emergency if other things fail

Fallenture: An act of a government when it destroys its own public property but blames the enemy of the country with the intention of starting a war [Contraction of fallen venture]

Fall guy: Someone who is punished for something wrong that somebody else has done, also termed scapegoat

Fall money: The money that a criminal sets aside to use in case he gets arrested

Falsies: The pads that a woman uses to make her breasts look bigger

False dawn: A situation in which you think that something good is going to happen but it does not happen

False flag: The activity of a government or organization to motivate the people to support or fight for an unfair war

Fancy man: A pimp who arranges customers for a prostitute

Fancy lover: A lover who is not serious in love and that is why he keeps on changing partners

Fancy woman: A man's mistress

Fanny: The female sex organ

Fantabulous: Wonderful

Faraway expression: An expression on your face that shows that your thoughts are far away from your present situation

Fart king: A man who is strong in speaking but weak in action

Fashionably late: The person who prefers reaching late giving an impression to others that he was held up with other work

Fast and furious: A film full of rapid action and sudden changes

Fatalist: Someone who believes that whatever happens in his life is decided by fate and he can not control or change it

Fat chance: A negligible prospect

Faux pas: An action that you take to do something good but something bad happens (Pronounced faw paa)

Feeflow: The vaginal saliva coming out during sexual secretion

Feel-good factor: The hopeful feeling about the future that is shared by many people

Feet of clay: The fault that you can not find out in first sight

Felch: A male homosexual who sucks out the semen of his partner

Fellatio: The sexual activity of sucking or licking a man's sex organ (Pronounced (fa-lei-shio)

Feminazi: A woman who supports feminism radically

Fence market: A market of stolen goods

Fender-bender: A person who stages a road accident and pretends that he has been injured so that he can claim compensation

Fever pitch: A very high level of excitement or activity

Fey: A person who is sensitive and rather mysterious and does not act in a very practical way

Fiasco: The work that does not succeed and therefore it embarrasses you

Fickle: A person who is changing his mind in an unreasonable way

Fifth column: A group of people living in his own country but working secretly to help the enemy of his country

Figment: Something that somebody has imagined and that does not really exist

Fight of Rhodesia: The fight to overthrow the government of minority community

Finger man: An informer to police

Finger smith: A pickpocket who is expert in stealing money

Finicky: A person who is too much worried about what he eats or wears

First-time stand: First time sex

First world: The rich industrial countries of the world

Fisting: The act of inserting hand into the sexual organ

Five-finger discount: Stealing something from a shop

Flabbergasted: Extremely surprised or shocked

Fladge: Sadomasochism – The act of torturing oneself in sex (Noun)

Flak-catcher: An employee to deal with the hostile comments or any offence on the behalf of the person or institution he is working for

Flamboyant: A confident and exciting person who can attract the attention of others

Flasher: The man who shows his sexual organ in public

Flash mob: A large number of people suddenly gathered at a particular place to perform an arbitrary action

Flashpoint: A situation or place in which violence or anger starts

Flea-bag: A soldier's sleeping bag

Flea market: An outdoor market in which second hand (used) good are sold at low price

Fleetcher: The father or mother who introduces their good-looking daughter to the acquainted persons for some financial benefits

Fellator: A woman who practices oral sex to a man

Flesh trade: Prostitution

Flexisexual: A man who is flexible in his sexual desire and so mostly he is attracted towards girls but sometimes he feels attracted towards boys also

Flighty: A woman who always keeps on changing her ideas, activities and partners without treating them seriously

Flip side: The side part of an idea, argument or action which is not so important

Floating voter: Someone who does not always vote for the same political party and so he has not decided which party he should vote for

Floozy: A woman in sexual relationships with many men

Flunky: A person who tries to please an important and powerful person by doing small jobs in order to gain some favor

Fly-by-night: The man who runs away without paying the money he had borrowed

Fly-flat: A victim of crime

Folk lore: The traditions and stories of a country or community

Fool's paradise: A false happiness that can not last longer

Forbidden fruit: Something that you are not allowed doing therefore it attracts you very much

Foreboding: A strong feeling that something unpleasant or dangerous is going to happen

Foreplay: A sexual activity of touching and kissing sexual organs

Forlorn: A lonely and unhappy person

Fortune hunter: A man who wants to become rich by marrying a rich woman

Foundling: A baby who has been abandoned by his parents

Fourth dimension: An experience that is outside normal human experience

Fourth estate: The press media and journalism

Frailty: The weakness in a person's character or morals

Frame-up: A situation when an innocent person is proven guilty of a crime by producing false evidence

Frantic: Someone who is not able to control his emotion because he is extremely frightened or worried about something

Freebooter: A man who takes part in a war in order to steal goods

Freemasonry: The friendship between the people who have the same profession or interests

French kiss: A kiss with one partner's tongue inserted in the other's mouth

French leave: The leave that you take without informing your senior

French letter: Condom

French sex: Oral sex

Freudian slip: The cleverness of saying something showing it a mistake but in reality you wanted to say that (Pronounced *froidian slip*)

Friday man: An employee who does all kind of work to his boss

Frogfinger: An extremely eccentric man who rapes his daughter

Front passage: The vagina

Frozen limit: Something that is going beyond limit therefore you can not tolerate that

Frump: A woman who wears unfashionable clothes

Fugly: A very ugly woman

Funk: Panic

Funkhole: A place to which one can go to avoid danger

Funny bone: The part of the elbow containing a very sensitive nerve that is painful if you hit it

Furtive: A person who is behaving in a way that shows that he wants to keep something secret and does not want to be noticed

Fusspot: A man who is often worried about unimportant things and is difficult to please

G

Gag: The one who is desperately eager for sexual intercourse

Gang-bang: The copulation with an individual by a group

Gangbuster: An officer of a law-enforcement agency in dealing with organized crime

Gatecrasher: A person who comes as an uninvited guest in your party and his intention is to just have food

Gentleman's: The toilet

Gigolo: The one who takes money from a rich woman to be her lover

Glad eye: An amorous glance

Glad hand: A cordial handshake

Glitch: A sudden brief irregularity or malfunction

Glitz: The glamour of show-business

Goatee: The hair that is grown on the chin of a male person

Go-getter: The one who is in the way of achieving success

Gongoozler: A person who stares idly at something

Goodish: A person who is trying to look good by wearing good clothes but in fact he is not good

Goody-goody: The one who admires you at your front but speaks all bad things behind

Goofy: Stupid

Googler: A person who spends much of his time searching things on Google

Goon: Thug

Goshing gosh: O my god! [An exclamatory expression – 'god' replaced with 'gosh']

Grandiloquent: The one who uses tough words or complicated sentences in speaking or writing to impress people

Grass widow: A woman who has been left by her husband for a long time

Grave crime: A big crime for which death punishment can be given

Graveyard shift: The odd working hour in an office somewhere at late night

Gravy: The unearned or unexpected money

Gravy train: The source of easy unearned financial profit

Gray area: An area of a subject or situation that is not clear or does not fit into a particular group and is therefore difficult to deal with

Greek love: Anal sex

Green horn: An illiterate person

Grog blossom: The redness of the nose caused by excessive drinking

Grope: To fondle a person's sexual organ or breasts

Grouch bag: A hidden pocket or purse carried in a concealed place for keeping the money safe

Ground zero reality: The bare truth that is not infected with any kind of lies at all

G spot: The part of the female body around front and back of her waist

G string: A thread-like panty worn by women similar to a thong but exposes much more

Guido: A socially unsophisticated person whose behavior is viewed as typically lower class

Gumgoozer: A tactical homosexual man who persuades his male friend in such a way that even the friend hates homosexuality still he makes him agree to for that

Gun moll: An armed woman

Gutter press: The activity of press media, when they publish a lot of shocking news about people's private lives rather than serious news

Grenade: An unattractive girl that you are using to approach a beautiful girl

H

Hairy eyeball: A look given with narrowed eyes indicating hostility or disapproval

Half-cut: The one who is fairly drunk

Half-humping: An act of sexual intercourse when a man withdraws his penis before ejaculation to prevent pregnancy, also called coitus interruptus

Hand-job: An act of masturbation being done by a woman to a man

Hanger-on: The one who tries to be friendly with famous persons in order to get advantage

Hanky-panky: The dishonest dealing

Happy-go-lucky: A person who doesn't care or worry about the future

Hard case: A person aggressively difficult to deal with

Hardhead: An obstinate person

Hard-on: An erection of the penis

Hard liner: The one who follows strict policy or attitude of something

Harem family: A family in which a man has many wives and children and they live together as seen in Arab world

Hatchet man: A hired killer

Headcase: A mentally unstable person

Heart quack: A mental or emotional instability caused by bad incidents

Heavy sugar: A large amount of money

Hedonist: The one who believes pleasure is the most important thing in life

Hell-bent: The one who is determined to do something even though the results may be bad

Head hunter: The one who collects the head of the people they kill

Hellacious: Terrific, awful

Hellmonk: The religious leader involved in extremely illicit activity

Henchman: A faithful supporter of a powerful person

Hen pecked: A man who obeys his wife for everything

Hibiswig: Swallowing the ejaculated semen during lovemaking

Hieros gamos: An ancient religious ceremony in which the couples gathered in an open place under a tree wearing partly or no clothes and they used to perform sex act chanting and remembering God

High-five: A gesture of celebration or greeting in which two people slap each other's hand with arms extended

High-hat: A snob who thinks he is better than other people because he is more intelligent

Highway man: A man who robs travelers on public roads

Hip-kiss: A kiss placed around the private part of the lover who is fully clothed

Hip-peeping: The considerably earlier erotic feeling in small children

Hit list: A list of people to be killed

Hit-man: A hired killer

Hogwash: Nonsense or rubbish talk or writing

Hoity-toity: A person with insincere behavior

Home-son-in-law: A man who stays at his wife's home

Home body: Someone who doesn't like to go out but enjoys spending time at home

Homesick: Someone who feels very sad because he is away from home and misses his family and friends

Honcho: A leader or boss

Honey-baby: A sweetheart

Honor killing: The act of killing somebody for the sake of the prestige

Hooker: The woman who grows in her career by offering sex to others

Hook-shop: A prostitute's house

Hot-air artist: A boaster – The one whose claims or promises sound impressive but have no real meaning or truth

Hot-pants: The erection (noun). *He's got the hot-pants.*

Humdinger: An excellent or remarkable person or thing

Hung up: Confused or bewildered

Hunk: A big, strong and attractive man

Hustler: A person who lives by stealing or other means

Hymen: A piece of skin that partly covers the opening of the vagina

I

Incest: The sexual crime between a brother and sister or a father and daughter

Indecent assault: A sexual attack on somebody but not rape

Individuality: An outer personality of a person that changes his look different from others

Identikit: The making of a picture with drawings of different features that can be put together to form the face of a person using description given by the witness

Identity crisis: The mental inability when a person does not recognize himself

Idée fixe: An idea that dominates the mind (Pronounced *eedei feex*)

Idiosyncrasy: A person's particular way of behaving or thinking

Iffy: A doubtful person

Illegit: An illegitimate child

Imbo: A gullible person who can be easily cheated

Illusionist: A person who spreads false idea or belief about something

Indie: An independent, theatre, film, or record company

Inertia: The lack of desire when a person does not want to change himself

Inferiority complex: A feeling that you are not as important or intelligent as other people, opposite to – superiority complex

Inginct: An act of a woman when she refuse having sex with her lover just to examine the patience and truthfulness of him. [Contraction of ingenious instinct]

Inside job: A crime committed by or with the help of someone working in a place where it took place

Inside stand: The placing of a gang member as one of the staff of a place to be robbed, in order to facilitate the robbery

Insular: The one who is interested in his own ideas

Insider: Someone who knows many secrets but he discloses that when right time comes

Intermittent: A woman's second boyfriend who she establishes physical relation with when her first boyfriend is out of station

Internee: The one who has been punished by the court to not go out of a specified place

Introspection: The careful examination of your thoughts, feeling and reasons

Insomnia: The condition of being unable to sleep in night

Item: The girlfriend

Itty-bitty: A very small thing

J

Jack pot: A large amount of money that is given to you as a prize in a game

Jackleg: A lawyer or preacher who is incompetent or unscrupulous

Jaffa: An infertile male

Jail bird: A criminal who goes to jail quite often

Jerk off: To masturbate

Jhakas: Something looking very nice

Jhol: A deception

Jilt: A woman who ends a romantic relationship with her lover in a sudden and unkind way

Jingle: Money in small coin

Jinx: A person or thing that brings bad luck

Jobsworth: A day trip, particularly one taken for pleasure and arranged from ones place of work

Johnson brother: A criminal

Jolt: A drink of liquor

Joy house: A brothel

Judgment Day: The day at the end of the world when God will judge everyone

Jugad: A makeshift of something brought to work for a temporary period of time

Juldy: Haste, hurry

Junkie: A drug addict

K

Kaffir: An unreliable person

Kangaroo court: A court in which the judgment is given in the favor of somebody without investigating the case properly

Keep: A woman who is living with a man without marriage

Key industry: The main industry which the county's economy is depending upon

Kick the bucket: To die (verb)

Kiddo: A kid; used as a familiar form of address to a man or woman

Kidlet: A small child

Kidvid: A television or video program made for children

Killjoy: The one who makes the people upset at the time of enjoyment, also called 'spoil-shot'

Kink: A sexually abnormal person

Kinsman: A far relative of yours from paternal link

Kiss-me-quick: The lock of hair that swings on the face of a woman making her more attractive, also called 'love lock'

Klepto: A thief (The abbreviation of kleptomaniac)

Knee-trembler: An act of sexual intercourse between people standing up

Knockers: A woman's breasts

Knock up: To make a woman pregnant (Verb)

Knocking shop: A place of prostitution

Knockover: Theft (Noun)

L

Lad: A group of male friends

Lady killer: A man who is very famous in women

Lady's man: A man who spends most of his time with women

Lalapaloosa: Something outstandingly good of its kind

Lallygag: Blowjob

Lame excuse: An excuse that can be caught and people can understand that you are telling lies

Lass-lorn: A broken-heart person who is suffering from pain because he is separated from his beloved

Lead: Male sexual potency, vigor

Lecherous: The one who is having strong or excessive sexual desire

Left field: A position away from the center of interest

Left-handed compliment: If somebody is admiring you with the intention of taunting – that is a left-handed compliment

Legal: A passenger who pays the exact fare to a taxi driver without any tip

Legart: Pornography

Lemon-game: Deception

Levity: The behavior that shows a lack of respect for something serious

Lexicographer: The one who writes a dictionary

Liaison: A secret sexual relationship

Libertine: A person who leads an immoral life and is interested in pleasure only

Light handed: A very active person who finishes his work fast

Ligger: The one who gatecrashes a party, a gatecrasher

Light skirt: A prostitute

Light hearted: The one who is intended to be amusing or easily enjoyable rather than too serious

Lilting English: The style of speaking English in a very sweet and melodious tone

Limbo: A situation in which you are not certain what you should do next because you are waiting for somebody else to make a decision

Lion hunter: A person who is too eager to develop his contacts with rich and influential people

Lipstick: A lesbian

Logomania: The act of talking too much that can show that the person is mentally ill

Loner: The one who likes to live alone

Loo: The toilet

Looky-frooky: A man who tempts a woman to see pornographic things acting innocently so that he can develop physical intimacy with her

Lorena Bobbitt: A woman who cuts the sexual organ of a man

Loss-leader: The one who sells goods at low price to attract customers

Louisiana loverboy: A married man who in looking for another female partner because he is not happy with his wife

Lounge lizard: A man who frequents fashionable parities in search of wealthy patroness

Love-lorn: A person who has got so much of pain in love

Low-heel: A woman readily agreeing to lie down for sexual intercourse

Lumber: A house where stolen property is hidden

Lunarfall: A perceived fall of white racist America's supremacy after the second time winning of Barack Obama

Lunchbox: The penis being more apparent by tightly fitting trousers

Lure-crime: The crime committed in sexual jealousy

Lurkman: A man who lives by stealing money

M

Masochist: A person who gets pleasure from giving pain to himself or others

Malarkey: Total nonsense or foolishness

Malky: A razor being used as a weapon

Mamma mia: O my god!

Mamzer: The one who is born of a prostitute

Man eater: A woman who is in sexual relationship with many men

March in Moscow: To visit a red-light area for the purpose of seeking enjoyment. In sentence – *Refrain yourself from having a march in Moscow*

Marge: A lesbian who takes the role of the passive or submissive partner

Marriage of convenience: A marriage that is made for practical, financial or political reasons and not for love

Marv: Marvelous, outstanding

Masher: A womanizer who makes indecent advances to women in public places

Mash note: A love letter

Matinee idol: A male actor who is very famous in women

Maverick: A man who does not behave or think like everyone else but he has independent unusual opinions

Mascot: An animal or toy or anything that people believe will bring them good luck

Malinger: The one who pretends to be ill to get rid of his work

Mazoola: Money

MCP: A male chauvinist, the abbreviation of 'male chauvinist pig'

Medico: A medical practitioner or student

Melancholia: A mental illness when the patient is depressed and worried about unnecessary fears

Mealy mouthed: The one who speaks very less

Mercenary: A man who fights for any group that offers payment

Mental block: The blocked state of mind when he is not able to think anything other than what he normally believes

Metrosexual: The average heterosexual man who is more concerned to his appearance of a gay man

Mexican shower: When a person does not have bath but wears perfume to hide his body smell

Midlife crisis: The worry, disappointment or lack of confidence that a person may feel in the middle of his life time

Mickey Mouse: Small, insignificant or worthless

Midas touch: Your ability when you can make a lot of money from any work you undertake

Middle leg: The penis

Migrant smuggling: The work of sending people abroad illegally

Midlife slicker: A person of middle age more inclined to mingling with women for developing romantic relationship

Mind-boggling: Mind-blowing

Mirage: An effect of hot air in desert that creates a misapprehension of water

Misery guts: A person who is always gloomy and complaining

Misotheist: The one who hates his religion and theological belief

Misper: A missing person

Miss: A miscarriage

Missionary position: A posture in sexual activity when a man lies on his female partner

Mitt-reader: A palmist or fortuneteller

Mixed blessing: Something that has both advantages and disadvantages

Mixet: A prostitute called by a married couple to give sexual pleasure to both a husband and wife at a time [Blend of mix it]

Mobster: The head of a mob involved in some bad activity

Mofo: Motherfucker (An abusive word)

Mokus: The depression caused by loneliness

Monkey-man: A weak and servile husband

Monkey parade: A promenade of young men and women in search of bed partners

Monoglot: Someone who speaks or knows only one language

Morose: A person who looks stupid because of his unhappy and bad tempered behavior

Moon-eyed: Drunk

Moonlighter: The man who makes a hurried departure by night because he is not able to pay the debts

Moonlight flit: An act of a moonlighter

Morning-after pill: A medicine that a woman can take to avoid pregnancy

Morning quarterback: The one who engages in criticism of something

Motorhead: A car or motorcycle enthusiast

Motormouth: The one who has no control on his mouth and so he speaks too much

Morning sickness: The vomiting sickness during pregnancy

Morning gift: The gift that a groom gives to his newly wedded wife

Moll: The concubine of a criminal man

Mobocracy: The dominance and power of a mob

Modesty snatcher: A man who outrages the modesty of women

Moonlight employee: A call girl or prostitute who hides her profession giving excuses of working in a night-shift call center

Monday blues: The tiredness that you feel on Monday after you enjoyed a weekend, and so, you do not want to work

Monomania: A strong concentration of interest upon one particular subject

Mouth honor: The act of giving respect not to the general people but to your own people or who you are familiar with

Mouthpiece: A lawyer

Mr. Big: The head of an organization

Mr. Clean: An honorable or incorruptible politician

Mucker: A vulgar person

Mucking: Euphemistic alteration of 'fucking'

Muffin tag: An attempt of a man to sit closed to a female traveler to feel the touch of her body

Munchausen's syndrome: The mental abnormality when a person pretends or tries to show that he is sick so that the people should pity him

Mummery: The meaningless festival or ceremony

Muff-diver: A man who practices cunnilingus

Mug shot: A photograph of a person in police records

Mumper: A beggar

Mumping: The acceptance by the police of small gifts or bribes from the trade-people

Munjon: An Australian Aborigine who has a little experience of white society and its customs

Murphy's Law: The supposed tendency of things to go wrong in a perverse or annoying way, also called 'Sod's law'

Myopic: The one who is not able to think outside his own situation

Mystery: A young and inexperienced girl to a city-life

Mythiciser: A person who creates false stories to make the people believe in religious incidents

N

Nab: To arrest someone in wrongdoing

Nah: No [Colloquial expression]

Nancy: An effeminate man

Nasty: A traumatic experience or concealed unpleasantness in a person's background

Natural call: The feel to go to toilet

Narcissism: The habit of admiring oneself too much

Neatnik: The one who is neat in his or her personal habits

Necrophagous: The one who eats the flesh of dead body

Necromancy: The practice of claiming to communicate with the dead by magic in order to learn about the future

Necrophilia: A kind of madness when a person wants to have sex with a dead body

Needle: A fit of irritation

Needle man: The man who injects himself with drugs

Nepotist: Someone who give unfair benefits to his own family when he is in a position of power

Neophyte: A person who is newly converted into a religion

Nerd: A foolish

Net-head: A person obsessed with using the internet

Newbie: A person new to some activity

New world: North and South America

Niagara shower: A woman's first sexual intercourse (Relating to *Niagara fall* in America)

Nickel nurser: A miser

Nig: A black person

Niggergram: A rumor or piece of gossip

Nilor: A man having no girlfriend

Nipper: Handcuffs

Nish: Nothing

Nitty-gritty: The reality or practical details of a matter

Nob: A person of wealth or high social position

Nobbins: The coins collected by a performer after an entertainment

Nodding funk: A situation full of confusions and disturbance when a man is not sure whether his female companion would allow him to have sex with her. In sentence – *I am in a nodding funk.*

Novice: A person who is new and has a little experience in a skill, job or situation

Non-denominational: The one who is not restricted to any religion

No-hoper: A useless or incompetent person

Nonce: A sexually mad person

Nooner: A daytime sex

Nope: No

Nork: An act of licking breasts in lovemaking

Nosy parker: A person who is too much interested in other people's affair

Nonage: The ancient time when human mind was not developed

Nostalgia: A feeling of sadness, which is mixed with pleasure and affection when you think of happy times in the past

Nocturnal emission: A dream full of sexual excitement in which a man ejaculates. A wet-dream

Notell: A motel used for illicit sexual assignations

No way: It is impossible

Numskull: A fool

Nuptial tie: The bondage of marriage

Nutcase: An eccentric or lunatic person

Nymphomania: Excessive sexual desire in women

O

Object soul: Someone who objects everything

Obsolete: A thing that is no longer in use because something new has been invented

Oedipus complex: An abnormality when a man starts feeling sexual desire for his mother or the mother feels the same for her son

Off: To kill (transitive verb). In sentence – *What if somebody offed you?*

Officious: The one who is too ready to tell the people what to do

Off money: Bribe

Okay: O.K.

Okey-dokey: O.K.

Old lady: wife

Omega trap: The sharp practice of a prostitute pretending to be your beloved

Ombudsman: A mediator between two parties to solve a dispute

One finger salute: To show the middle finger of the hand to someone as a matter of disgust

One-night stand: A sexual relationship of one night

One-way pockets: The pockets of a miser person

Onion: A woman with whom several men have intercourse one after another

Oomph: Sex appeal

Open faced: The person whose thought can be easily understood by seeing his face

Operation false flag: The activity of a government or organization to motivate the people to support or fight for an unfair war

Organ: The penis

Orphan paper: A bad cheque

Ort: The anus

Out spoken: Someone who says exactly what he thinks, even if it shocks or offends people

Out law: A person who has done something illegal and is hiding to avoid being caught

Overhung: The one who is suffering from a hang-over

Overjolt: The overdose of a drug

P

Pacifist: The one who believes in peace and refuses to fight in war

Pan: The face

Panacea: Something that will solve all the problems of a particular situation (Pronounced *panaasia*)

Pandora box: The one problem, that is so sensitive and dangerous that if you go to solve it, it will open so many other problems

Panhandler: A street beggar

Pantsing: The action of pulling down someone's trousers or underpants as a practical joke

Paper hanger: The one who passes forged or fraudulent cheques

Paper horse: A person or a team who fails to accomplish a certain task of your expectation

Paparazzi: A photographer who follows famous people around in order to get interesting photos

Paramour: A lover of a married woman

Parlor-house: An expensive type of brothel

Passive debt: The money that you had given to somebody as a loan but you can not get it back

Paternity suit: A court case intended to prove who the father of a child is

Payola: A bribe or other secret payment to induce someone to use his or her influence for promoting a commercial product

Peanut: Someone small or unimportant

Peck's bad boy: A wild, unmanageable, or mischievous boy

Pedant: Someone who is proud of his knowledge or learning

Pederast: A man too much inclined to have sex with small children

Pedophilia: The abnormality of having sex with small children

Pee-peeping: The abnormal activity of a man intending to see a woman using toilet

Pegging: The act of sexual activity when a woman uses strap-on dildo to penetrate into her male partner

Penman: A forger

Pep talk: False courageous talk

Persecution complex: A type of mental illness in which one feels that the other people are trying to harm him

Permissive: A person who shows a free behavior in sexual matter

Pervert: A person with abnormal sexual behavior in which he or she may be interested in animal-sex or some other strange activities

Pervics: A person who gets bore from things easily

Petticoat government: The dominance of a wife on her husband

Philogynist: A man who likes women very much

Picasso: A desperate and restless person who is trying to learn something with unstable mind

Pig parliament: The blind, careless and cunning government of a country which is not willing to do anything for the betterment of the people

Pimp: The person who arranges customers for a prostitute

Pink chamber: A good looking female staff appointed in an office to keep all the male staffs energized

Pink prescription: The immoral and illegal practice of a doctor when he gives the wrong information about a disease intending to earn more money from you

Pipecam: A criminal act of a person when he captures the nude video of someone's private life to sell it online (Noun)

Pip-pip: Good bye

Pirate: To form a casual friendship with someone with a view to sexual intercourse

Pisher: Someone who urinates in bed while sleeping

Pissing contest: A futile or purposeless contest

Piss-up: A complete mess-up

Pixilated: A person who is mildly insane

Pizzazz: Vitality or zest

Placebo: The substance which looks like a medicine, is given to a patient who does not need medicine and so the substance has no physical effect

Placer: Someone who deals in stolen goods

Platonic love: The love with no involvement of sex

Play boy: A rich man who spends his time enjoying himself

Pledgitive: A person who abandons their pledged religious life and joins worldly life [Contraction of pledge fugitive]

Plonk: A female police officer

Pluperfect: (An adjective used as an intensifier) – *What the pluperfect have you got to do?*

Plutocracy: A government by the richest people of the country

Plutish: A person involved in plutocracy

Plutomania: The desire to earn excessively more and more money

Pocket billiards: The act of masturbation keeping the hand in trouser pocket (Noun)

Pocketbook: The vagina

Poena: An exercise given as punishment to a child

Poindexter: An over-industrious student

Pointy-head: An intellectual

Poker-faced: The one having a humorless expression

Politricks: Politics regarded as being characterized by dishonesty or self-interest [Blend of politics and trick]

Polygamy: The custom of having more than one wife at a time

Polyandry: The custom of having more than one husband at a time

Pom-pom: Sexual intercourse

Ponce: A man who lives off prostitute's earning

Poodle-faker: A man who cultivates a female group or society for personal advancement

Poopsy: A sweetheart or girlfriend

Poopy suit: A one-piece garment providing protection for the whole body

Pork barrel: The funds obtained by political influence

Porn picrix: A person who edits a normal photo to look like nude and sells online illegally

Portuguese parliament: A noisy discussion when everybody talks and nobody listens

Position 69: A posture in sexual activity in which a man and woman can lick each other's sexual organ at a time

Position 99: Anal sex

Position fireturn: A posture when a woman positions her body in such a way that the man can have vaginal and anal intercourse with her at a time

Postal: To behave violently as a result of stress. In sentence – *Stop going postal like this.*

Postilion: The anal stimulation of a partner with the finger

Pot companion: The person who accompanies you at the time of drinking alcohol

Pot belly: A person with big stomach

Potless: Poor

Pot-smoker: A marijuana smoker

Power monger: Someone with the greed of acquiring power

Prankster: A person who creates troubles for others and enjoys doing that

Presentiment: A feeling that something unpleasant is going to happen

Prick-teaser: The woman who attracts her lover but finally refuses to get along physically. Also called 'vagina drop'

Private: The genital

Profanity: Speaking abusive or insulting words

Prop doctor: The doctor who misguides their patients to earn more money

Propeller: Someone with an obsessive interest in computers or other technology

Psychodrama: A way of treating mentally ill people by encouraging them to act events from their past to help them understand their feelings

Psychopath: A person suffering from serious mental illness that causes him to behave in a violent way

Pubic hair: The hair near the sexual organs, also called 'pubes'

Pubic symphysis: The surrounding area of a woman's vagina full of sexual sensitivity

Pudendum: Vagina

Pukka: Excellent

Pull a job: To commit a robbery (Verb)

Pump metal: To shoot bullets

Punk-ass: A good-for-nothing person

Purler: Something excellent or outstanding

Purse proud: The one who is proud of his wealth

Push money: The commission on sold items

Put one's face on: To apply cosmetic make up

Putty medal: An appropriately worthless reward for insignificant service

Pyro: A pyromaniac person

Q

Queer bashing: the rape of a homosexual

Queer Street: Difficulty or trouble. In sentence – *I am in Queer Street*

Quickie: A sexual act of very short time

Quiv: A girl who is more willing to have physical relation with her boyfriend in first meeting

Quandong: Someone who looks after his or her own interest disreputably

Quim: The vulva

R

Race suicide: When a married couple decides to not give birth to any child in order to control the population of the country – that is race suicide

Rain maker: A highly successful person

Rampsman: Someone who commits robbery with violence

Ramrod: An erect penis

Rap sheet: A police record

Rapture: A feeling of extreme pleasure and happiness

Rat pack: A disorderly mob of youths

Raunchy: A person who is very naughty in sexual activity

Rave party: A rapturous and illicit party with loud music and dance

Raver: Someone who is passionately enthusiastic about a particular thing

Razor mouth: A person who does not let other people talk because he cuts them short before they complete saying

Razzle-dazzle: The excitement or noisy publicity

Reactionary: Someone who does not like his social setup

Recluse: Someone who lives alone for religious reason

Red: An anarchist or extremely socialist person

Red-light area: A part of town for prostitution

Red rampage: The act of having sex with a woman who is having menstruation

Red tape: The official rules that is more complicated than necessary and prevent things from being done quickly

Renegade: The one who opposes and lives outside of a group that he used to belong to

Rental-behind: A male homosexual prostitute

Resilient: The one who is able to feel better quickly after something unpleasant of shocking thing has happened in his life

Retard: A mentally retarded person

Reverse manipulation: The act when you make somebody so anxious that he will do the work that will benefit you

Rib-joint: A brothel

Rimming: The sexual act of licking the anus of a partner, also called 'anilingus'

Rip-off: To swindle (verb)

Rise: An erection of the penis

Rivol: Your husband's another wife is your rivol

Roach: A cockroach

Road hog: An inconsiderate driver or cyclist

Roller: A thief who robs drunken people. A prostitute who steals from her clients

Rolling stone: The one who keeps on changing his job, opinion or ideas

Rotten apple: A man who is very dangerous and harmful to the group he is in because he misguides other

Rough diamond: The one who has many good qualities but he does not look polite and educated

Rough spin: A misfortune or piece of bad luck

Rough tongued: A person with bad manner of speaking

Rough trade: The homosexual prostitution

Rubber: A condom, also called 'French letter'

Rubicon: A point at which you can not change the decision that you have already taken or you can not step back also

Ruckus: A commotion or disturbance

S

Sack rat: A person who spends too much time in bed

Sacrilegious: The one who treats a holy thing or place without respect

Sadistic: The person who gets pleasure from hurting other people

Safe: A condom

Salad days: The time when you are young and enjoy a lot because neither you have any worry nor any experience

Saltash luck: A miserable task that involves getting wet while doing

Sanitary napkin: A tampon – The thick piece of soft material that women wear outside their body to absorb the blood during the period

Satellite: A person who tries to be friendly with a famous person in order to get some advantage

Saturday-night secretary: A female secretary who is working in a company keeping a romantic relationship with her boss

Scamster: The one who is very clever and dishonest in planning of making money

Scandalous: A person who gets involved in a bad or immoral activity to be famous

Scapegoat: A person who is blamed for something bad that somebody else has done

Scaramouch: A coward man who admires himself a lot

Scarlet woman: A woman who is in relationship with many men

Scatterbrain: The one who forgets things and cannot think in organized way

Schizophrenia: A mental illness when a person is unable to link his thoughts, emotion and behavior that makes him unstable with reality and personal relationship

Schiz: A person suffering from schizophrenia

Schlimazel: A person who is consistently unlucky. (Pronounced – *shlimozl*)

Scorcher: A very hot day

Scrag: To manhandle or treat roughly (Verb)

Screenager: A young person who is at ease using computer technology with new media features

Scum: Semen

Scumbag: A condom

Scuzzy: Someone disgusting in appearance

Secko: A sexual pervert

Second banana: A supporting comedian

Second god: Money

Seducer: A man or woman who persuades somebody for sex

Self pleaser: A selfish person

Self pollute: To masturbate (verb)

Seventh heaven: A state joyfulness. In sentence – *My friend is in seventh heaven.*

Sexational: A thing which is sexually sensational

Sexilent: A very sexy woman

Sexpert: An expert who gives advices on sexual matter

Shagtastic: A very attractive woman

Shake-down: A forced contribution

Shambolic: Something which is extremely disorganized (Adjective)

Shanghai: To put someone in an awkward situation by trickery (verb)

Sharp practice: The act of cheating somebody

Sharpie: A person with extremely provocative style of dress and hair

Shellback: A person of long experience and reactionary views

She-male: A passive male homosexual

Shirker: A person who puts off his work

Shonk: Someone engaged in illegal business activities

Shoo-fly: A policeman in plain clothes whose job is to watch and report on other police officers

Shop lifting: Stealing goods from a shop

Short-arm: An inspection of the penis for sexual disease or other infection (Noun)

Short time: A brief stay in a hotel for sexual purposes

Shotgun marriage: The marriage that takes place quickly because the bride is already pregnant

Shunt: A road accident

Shutter-bug: An enthusiastic photographer

Sickstick: A mild pervert man who enjoys penetrating his anus with sticks

Signora: Madam

Signora Effect: The tiredness or weakness caused after having too much of sex

Silly billy: A foolish or feeble minded person

Silent majority: The large numbers of people in a country who think the same but don't express their views publically

Silver spoon: Prosperity or richness

Silver tongue: The one who praises others dishonestly or talks sweetly to get some benefits

Sin city: A city of recklessness and vice

Sitter: Someone employed to sit in a bar and encourage other patrons to buy drinks

Size zero: The look of a slim woman

Slanderer: A person who gives a malicious, false, and injurious statement about another

Skell: A homeless person who sleeps in a subway

Skid row: A part of town frequented by vagrants and alcoholic people

Skin-flick: An explicitly pornographic film

Skin house: An illegal theatre showing pornographic films

Skint: A person without any money left

Skirt chaser: A male person who keeps on looking for new girls to go to bed with

Skirt patrol: A search for female sexual partners

Skull-buster: Very challenging problem

Slacker: An aimless young person with lack of ambition

Slaphead: A bald person

Sledging: An attempt by the fielders to upset a batsman's concentration

Sleeping dictionary: A foreign woman with whom a man has a sexual relationship and from whom he learns some words of her language

Slicker: A smart of sophisticated person

Slips between hand and mouth: The difficulties someone is facing in earning his living. In sentence – *He is facing a lot of slips between hand and mouth.*

Slip-point flickering: The activity of a man looking at a girl in an office without her notice

Slit: The vulva

Sloane Ranger: A fashionable and conventional upper-middle-class young person

Slob: A lazy, dirty and untidy person

Slush fund: A reserve fund used for political bribery

Smart mouth: A person who is good at giving retort

Smasher: A sexually attractive man or woman

Smasheroo: A great success

Smelly: Something which is arousing suspicion (Adjective)

Smoke-up: An official notice that a student's work is not up to the required standard

Snafu: An utter confusion or chaos

Snarf: To eat or drink quickly or greedily (Verb)

Snifty: Haughty or disdainful

Snit: A state of agitation

Snollygoster: An unprincipled person in politics or other group

Snobby: If you think you are better than other people because you are more intelligent, and so, you give importance to high social class, you will be called snobby

SnM: Sadomasochism – The enjoyment from hurting somebody and being hurt in sexual activity

Snooper: Detective

SOB: Son of a bitch (Abusive word)

Sob sister: A female journalist who writes sentimental articles. An actress who plays sentimental roles

Soco: A police officer trained to examine senses of crime for forensic evidence

Sodawater effort: An effort which ends before bringing any result

Sodophilia: An abnormal inclination for anal sex

Sodomission: A permission that a man asks from his female partner to go for anal sex

Soft soap: Flattery

Soft touch: A person who can be easily manipulated

Soldier's farewell: An abusive farewell

Sollicker: Something very big

Sometimey: An unstable person

Sourpuss: A miserable person

Souvenir: A thing that you buy to remind you a place or an occasion

Spacy: Someone in the state of euphoria or disorientation (Adjective)

Sparrow brain: A person with limited intelligence

Sparrow cop: A police who is assigned low-grade duties such as patrolling parks

Speak easy: An illegal alcohol shop

Spear-carrier: An actor with a walk-on part. An unimportant participant

Spec: A commercial speculation of future success or gain (Noun)

Spiffing: Excellent

Spinster: A woman who is getting older but not willing to marry

Splendiferous: Magnificent

Spliced: Married

Split personality: The mental disorder when a person gets a fit of anger that makes him forget himself and he starts behaving in a very violent way

Spod: An obsessively studious person

Sophist: The one who is very clever in speaking or able to understand difficult or complicated ideas

Sponger: The one who gets money and food from other people without doing anything

Spoil-shot: A person who makes you suddenly sad while you are enjoying

Squarehead: Someone with no criminal convictions

Squaresville: A conventional place or institution, also called 'cubesville'

Squeaky clean: Something above criticism (Adjective)

Squillionaire: A multi-millionaire

Stable: A prostitute permanently fixed for a man or organization

Staff-wallah: A noncombatant army officer

Standover man: The one who uses intimidatory tactics

Star prisoner: The one who has gone to jail for the first time

Steaming: The action of a gang rushing through a public place robbing bystanders or passengers by force of numbers

Stem-winder: A forceful energetic person

Sticky wicket: A difficult situation

Stoic: The one who is able to suffer pain or trouble without complaining

Straight: The one who is not homosexual

Strap-hanger: A standing passenger in a bus

Strip tease: A form of entertainment in a bar or club, when a performer removes his or her clothes in sexually exciting way in front of an audience

Stud: A man of great sexual prowess

Subdeb: A girl who will soon come out as a debutante

Substitute: A woman's second boyfriend who she establishes physical relation with when her first boyfriend is out of station, also called 'intermittent'

Sugar daddy: A rich older man who flirts with much younger woman

Sumbitch: Son of a bitch (Abusive word)

Supergrass: A criminal who informs the police about the activity or other criminals for less punishment

Sunset trip: A trip of roaming around with your lover especially in the evening after getting out of office

Suspended sentence: A punishment given to a criminal in a court of law which means that he will only go to prison if he commits another crime within a particular period of time

Suspended animation: A feeling that you cannot do anything because you are waiting for something to happen

Suspended hooker: A prostitute who posts her profile on matrimonial websites to attract clients

Swallow: A woman employed in an intelligence service to seduce men for the purpose of espionage

Swifty: The one who thinks and acts quickly

Swindle sheet: A document of an account containing fraudulent claims

Swinger: The one who engages in group sex or partner-swapping

Swiss itch: A method of drinking spirits licking salt and lemon

Switcheroo: A surprising change or unexpected twist in a story (Pronounced – swicharoo)

Switch-hitter: A bisexual person

Sycophant: A servile flatterer

Sysop: A system operator assisting in the running of computer network

T

Tampon: A piece of cotton material that a woman puts inside her innerwear to absorb blood during her period

Table-ender: An act of copulation on a table

Tafia: Any supposed network of prominent or influential people which is strongly nationalistic

Tailgate: To drive too close behind another vehicle (Verb)

Tatty-bye: Good bye

Tea room: A public lavatory used for homosexual act by gay people

Technoterate: A technically literate person with good knowledge of technology

Tedonist: The people who believe that filling stomach and fulfilling sexual desire is the only purpose of human life on earth [Resembling to hedonist]

Teeny-bopper: A young teenager who follows the latest fashion in clothes and music

Teetotaler: The one who doesn't drink wine or take any narcotic things

Teleology: If you think there is a purpose behind whatever is happening in the world – this thinking is called teleology

Tender hearted: A person with a very soft heart

Tenderloin: A district of a city where vice and corruption are common

Tender feeling: Love

Theocracy: The government of a country by religious leaders

Theorist: The one who develops ideas and principles about a particular subject in order to explain why things happen or exist

Thousand-miler: A dark shirt of yours which you do not wash regularly because it does not show the dirt

Tinseltown: Hollywood

Tiswas: A state of nervous agitation or confusion (Pronounced – tiswoz)

Third degree: The act of threats or violence to get information from somebody

Tochan: The unnecessary lecture or instructions

Tomcat: To pursue women for the sake of sexual gratification (Verb)

Threesome: A sexual act with the involvement of three persons, also called 'troilism'

Thunderbox: A toilet

Time pleaser: Opportunist

Titty wank: The act of a female, when she rubs her nipples in the sexually sensitive area of a man to stimulate him for sex

Torch: To set fire in order to claim insurance money

Toddler: A child who is learning to walk

Torpedo: An armed criminal

Tosser: A female erotic dancer

Touch-me-not: The one who does not like to mingle with people and keeps himself reserved

Toy boy: A male lover or husband who is younger than his beloved or wife

Transsexual: The one who behaves like a member of opposite sex or who wants to change his sex

Trickster: Cheater

Trojan horse: A person or thing that is used to deceive an enemy in order to achieve a secret purpose

Trollies: Women's underpants

Trouble and strife: Wife

Trum: The penis of considerably large size [Derivation of tumescent]

Tuft hunter: A person who is eager to make contacts with rich and powerful people

Turf war: The fight among criminals over the right to operate an area

Tumescent: A man with large sexual organ

Turn coat: The one who changes his political party or religious group very frequently

Twirltag: To remarry ones ex wife or husband. (Verb – *Do you think you should twirltag this year*)

Twist: A woman

Two-pot screamer: Someone who becomes easily drunk

U

Uglies: Depression

Under employment: The situation when the people are not getting the job that can make full use of their skills and abilities so they start doing the jobs of lower standard

Under-handed: Fraud

Undersexed: A person with weak sexual power

Upper story: The human head

Upstart: A newly rich person

Usurer: The one who lends money to people at unfairly high rates of interests (Pronounced yoozarər)

Utopia: An imaginary place or state in which everything is perfect

U tuber: Someone who searches for explicit videos on U Tube or internet

U turn: The time when you completely change your policy which was not expected by the people

U wear: Underwear

Uxorious: The one who loves his wife very much

V

V: Vagina

Vagabond: A person who has no homes so he travels from place to place

Vainglorious: A man who is too proud of his abilities or achievements

Vanguard: The leaders of a movement in a society

V-drop: Vagina drop – The activity of a woman to attract her lover but refuse to have physical relation at the time of sexual excitement

Veejay: The one who presents a music program on television

Veep: The vice-president

Venereal disease: Relating to sexual disease

Versatile: Someone who is able to do many things

Vicky-verky: Vice versa

Vidiot: A habitual and obsessed watcher of television or player of video games

Virginia jaundice: A common but persistent thinking of some men to get married with virgin girls only

Virility: The sexual power in men

Voluptuous: A woman with large breasts and hip

Voracious: The one who eats too much

Voyeur: The one who gets pleasure by secretly watching other people having sex

W

Wag: A female partner of a male celebrity

Wallflower: A neglected or socially awkward person

Wanderlust: Someone who keeps travelling from places to places

Wanker: A masturbator man

Wankered: Very intoxicated

Warez: The illegal copies of commercial software and its distribution (Pronounced weərz)

Watering cabin: A place where alcoholic refreshment is available

Weak bladder: The one who urinates frequently

Well-hung: A man with a large genital

Wetback: The one who enters the US illegally

Wet blanket: 1 A friend of yours who has stopped talking to you. 2 The one who is not enthusiastic about anything

Wetcourse: Sexual act during bath

Wet dream: A dream full of sexual excitement that leads to ejaculation

Wetleg: A self-pitying person

White ant: A person who fails in their sanity or intelligence, a synonym of 'pledgitive'

White elephant: A thing that it is useless and no longer needed for you because you spend a lot of money in order to maintain it

White flagger: A person who easily accepts defeat and stops fighting

White hope: The hope that you think cannot bring success

White knight: A company that comes to the aid of another facing an unwelcome take-over bid

White lie: The lie that people can understand easily

White night: The night that you passed without sleeping or could not sleep

White slave: A woman who is forced to become a prostitute

Whizz-boy: A pickpocket

Wife swapping: The act of exchanging wife with someone else's in a party or club

Wisdom tooth: Any of the four large teeth at the back of the mouth that do not grow until you are an adult

Windbag: A person who talks a lot but says little of value

Winkler: The one who assists in the eviction of tenants

Wiseacre: The one who shows that he is wise but in fact he is not

Womanizer: A man who persuades women

Woofits: A feeling that you are unwell which is just in your head

Workaholic: A person who works very hard

Working girl: A prostitute

Worldly minded: The one who has a lot of experience and knows how he should live in the world

Wowser: An extremely prudish person

Wrongside injector: A doctor with a weak caliber who gets sensual while treating female patients

X

Xenophobe: The one who hates foreigners

X rated: A film or something that people under 18 are not allowed to see

X factor: If you have some special quality than usual for a purpose – that is X factor

X-rayser: A sexually obsessed man who looks at women with piercing eyes

Y

Yardie: An African man engaged in drug-related organized crime

Yellow-belly: A coward

Yellow peril: A strong mindset of a person when he feels that without following the western culture the other countries cannot progress

Yellow journalism: The activity of press media making the news sensational to attract viewers

Yenta: A nagging woman

Yo-yo English: The bad and corrupt English being used by some Africans and other nationals

Z

Zigzig: Sexual intercourse

Zillion: A very large number

Zillionaire: A very rich person

Zinger: Something outstandingly good of its kind

Zionist: The racist and fascist white American

Zipdown: Sexual intercourse

Zipless: A person very passionate about sexual encounter

Zoanthropy: The madness when a person starts feeling that he is an animal

Zombie: The one who seems only partly alive without any feeling or interest in what is happening

This is a dictionary of slang, so you got only and nearly slang words which are accepted and being used in English. For general words, I have compiled another dictionary titled ENGLISH WORD POWER.

Niranjan Jha Showman
+91-9561450045
cromosys@yahoo.com
Mumbai, India
facebook.com/cromosys

NIRANJAN JHA SHOWMAN

Founder - Niranjan Jha Showman

Education and Technology Research Center

Patankar Park, Nallasopara (W), Mumbai. +91-9561450045

Education, Technology, Publication, Healthcare, Newsmedia, Realtor, Filmmaking

www.facebook.com/cromosys

Cromosys Publication
Teach
Yourself
German
NIRANJAN JHA SHOWMAN

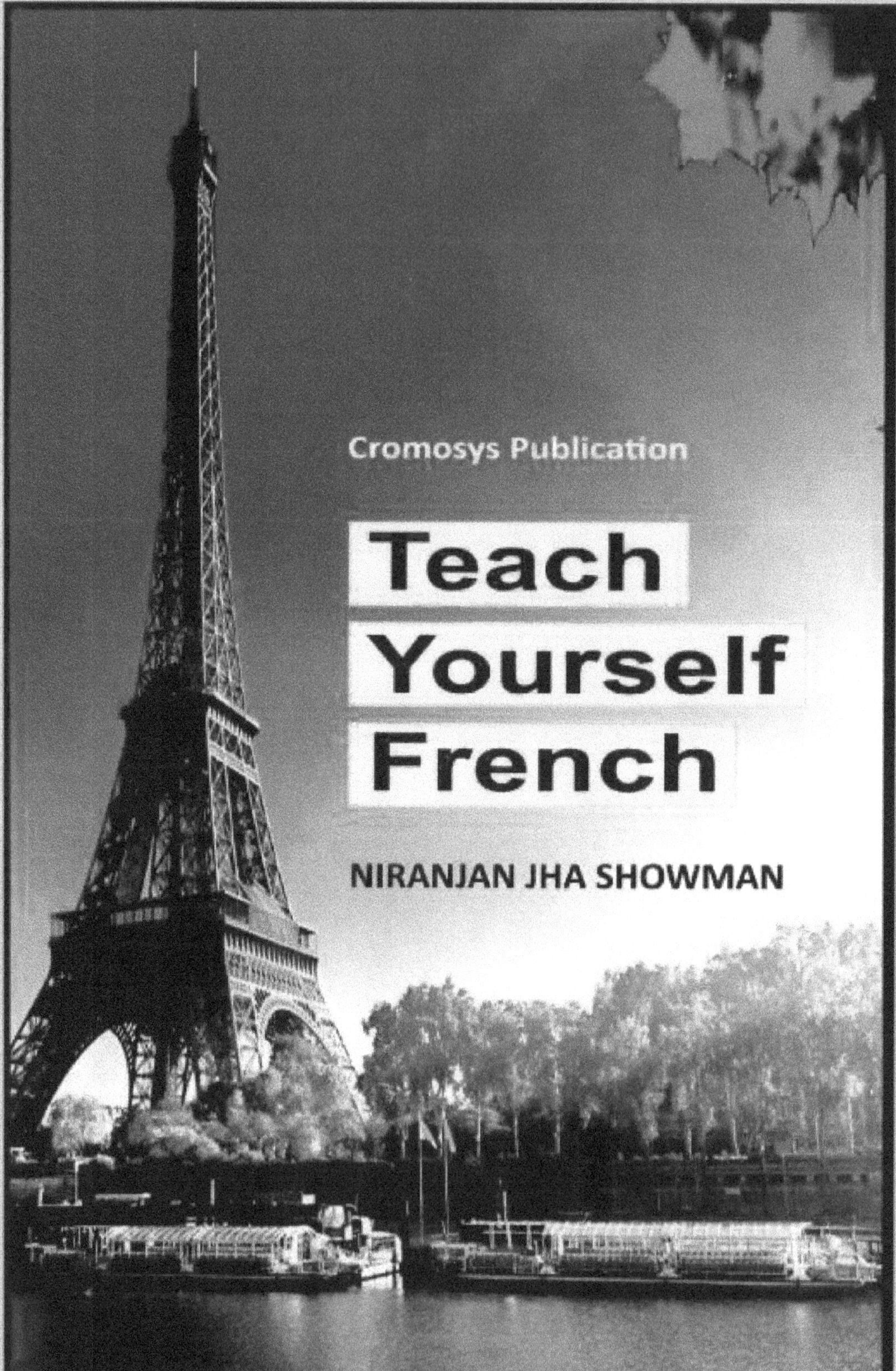
Cromosys Publication
Teach
Yourself
French
NIRANJAN JHA SHOWMAN

Cromosys Publication
Teach
Yourself
Spanish
NIRANJAN JHA SHOWMAN

Cromosys Publication

English
Voice
Accent and
Pronunciation

NIRANJAN JHA SHOWMAN

Teach
Yourself
Autodesk
MAYA
Cromosys Publication
NIRANJAN JHA SHOWMAN

Cromosys Publication
Teach
Yourself
Autodesk
3ds Max
NIRANJAN JHA SHOWMAN

Cromosys Publication
CRIMINAL FACTORY
NIRANJAN JHA SHOWMAN

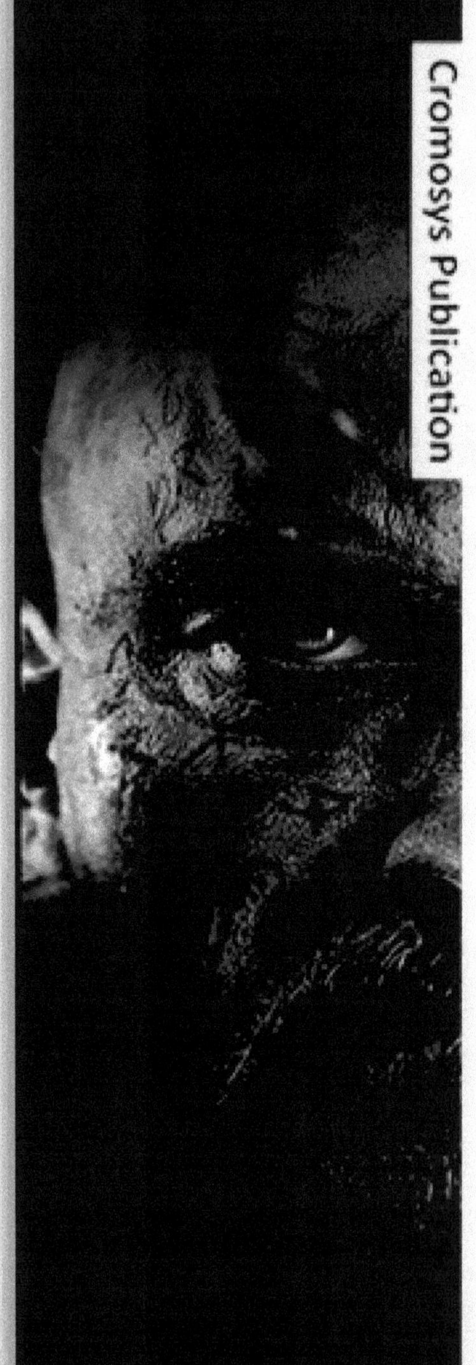

Cromosys Publication
FOCAL DISASTER
NIRANJAN JHA SHOWMAN

Cromosys Publication
Your talents will not help you succeed without your skill of using them.
NIRANJAN JHA SHOWMAN
BE
MILLIONAIRE
LIKE
ME

Extracts
from the Register
of Copyrights

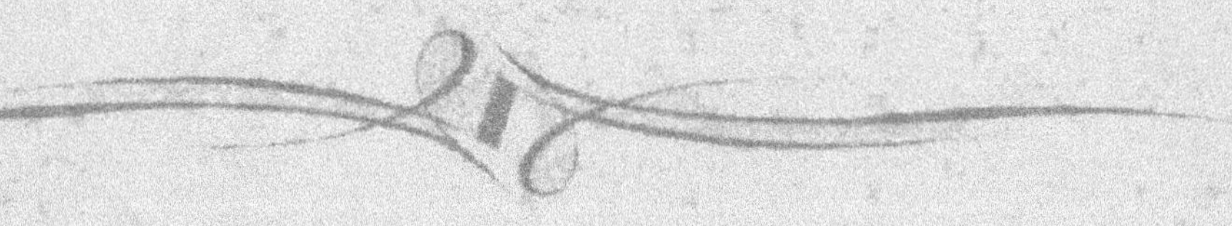

Dated : 17/08/2022

1.	Registration Number	:	**T-98712-2022**
2.	Name, address and nationality of the applicant	:	NIRANJAN JHA SHOWMAN, CROMOSYS PUBLICATION, 001, JAYSATYAM, PATANKAR ROAD, NALLASOPARA (W), MUMBAI, MAHARASHTRA - 401203. INDIAN
3.	Nature of the applicant's interest in the copyright of the work	:	AUTHOR
4.	Class and description of the work	:	LITERARY / BOOK
5.	Title of the work	:	**English Dictionary of Modern Slang**
6.	Language of the work	:	ENGLISH
7.	Name, address and nationality of the author and if the author is deceased, date of his decease	:	NIRANJAN JHA SHOWMAN, CROMOSYS PUBLICATION, 001, JAYSATYAM, PATANKAR ROAD, NALLASOPARA (W), MUMBAI, MAHARASHTRA - 401203. INDIAN
8.	Whether the work is published or unpublished	:	UNPUBLISHED
9.	Year and country of first publication and name, address and nationality of the publisher	:	N.A.
10.	Years and countries of subsequent publications, if any, and names, addresses and nationalities of the publishers	:	N.A. SAME AS ABOVE
11.	Names, addresses and nationalities of the owners of various rights comprising the copyright in the work and the extent of rights held by each, together with particulars of assignments and licences, if any	:	
12.	Names, addresses and nationalities of other persons, if any, authorised to assign or licence of rights comprising the copyright	:	N.A.
13.	If the work is an 'Artistic work', the location of the original work, including name, address and nationality of the person in possession of the work. (In the case of an architectural work, the year of completion of the work should also be shown).	:	N.A.
14.	If the work is an 'Artistic work', whether it is registered under the Designs Act 2000 if yes give details.	:	N.A.
15.	If the work is an 'Artistic work', capable of being registered as a design under the Designs Act 2000.whether it has been applied to an article though an industrial process and ,if yes ,the number of times it is reproduced.	:	N.A.
16.	Remarks, if any	:	

Diary Number : 9765/2020-DF/T
Date of Application : 25/07/2021
Date of Receipt : 25/07/2021

DEPUTY REGISTRAR OF COPYRIGHTS

www.ingramcontent.com/pod-product-compliance
Lightning Source LLC
Chambersburg PA
CBHW040149110726
48005CB00018B/2703